YOUR KNOWLEDGE HAS VALUE

AF138456

- We will publish your bachelor's and master's thesis, essays and papers

- Your own eBook and book - sold worldwide in all relevant shops

- Earn money with each sale

Upload your text at www.GRIN.com
and publish for free

The impact of Social Media #EndSARS Nigerian Youth Activism for Police Accountability in Nigeria

Adegboyega Daniel Eniola

Bibliographic information published by the German National Library:

The German National Library lists this publication in the National Bibliography; detailed bibliographic data are available on the Internet at http://dnb.dnb.de.

ISBN: 9783346840592
This book is also available as an ebook.

© GRIN Publishing GmbH
Nymphenburger Straße 86
80636 München

Print and binding: Books on Demand GmbH, Norderstedt, Germany
Printed on acid-free paper from responsible sources.

The present work has been carefully prepared. Nevertheless, authors and publishers do not incur liability for the correctness of information, notes, links and advice as well as any printing errors.

GRIN web shop: https://www.grin.com/document/1336698

THE IMPACTS OF SOCIAL MEDIA ON THE #ENDSARS NIGERIAN YOUTHS ACTIVISM FOR POLICE ACCOUNTABILITY IN NIGERIA

By

ADEGBOYEGA DANIEL ENIOLA

Department of Mass Communication
University of Lagos, Akoka

ABSTRACT

This article reveals how Nigerian youths reacted to the tragic shooting of a Nigerian man by agents of the Special Anti-Robbery Squad, a unit of the Nigerian Police Force (NPF), in Delta State, Nigeria. Between November 2017 and October 2020, series of vibrant online and physical protests organized under the hashtag of #EndSARS campaign was staged against the operation of the Special Anti-Robbery Squad (SARS) for their abuse of power which indicates police brutality in Africa's most populous country. Thus, this article examined the factors that led to the outburst of the #EndSARS protest as a strategic means for seeking police accountability, that represent the youths capacity to plan, organize, execute, assemble and persuade the Nigerian Government to act and the impact of the mass action on policing and law enforcement in Nigeria. The methodology postulated for this study consists of a qualitative analysis of tweets between September 11 and October 11, 2020. The findings revealed the various strategies Nigerian Youths used to shape the activism against police brutality and influence the Government's decision to eradicate the SARS Unit of the Nigeria Police Force.

Keywords: Protest, Social Media, Activism, SARS, Nigeria.

Introduction

Since the innovative inception of digitalization in the modern world, especially in Africa, the use of social media as a means of communication has found expressions in political, economic and social aspects of humans engagements. Social media has gained so much admiration amongst individuals due to the available means of self-expression, interaction and communication, especially on Twitter, Facebook, WhatsApp, and Instagram. This is because pictures and videos allow others to glance into users' everyday lives, interests, and personal experience. The use of social media has aided social groups and campaigns to survive in the dissemination of information and communication in the world of today. It has also impacted the dissemination of government communications, decisions, and policy making processes through their various official handles on social media platforms.

In respect to the phenomenon of the Nigerian youths #EndSARSprotests, which was organized to protest against police brutality and call for conscious policy and policing reforms in the country, social media platforms specifically twitter, was maximized by the youths' in Nigeria to vibrantly protest both online and offline against police brutality that consequently persuaded the Nigerian government decisions in its security and social policy making. This phenomenon called for rigorous academic debate in regards to the efficacy of social media platforms as tools that citizens can maximize to influence government policies and decision making processes in Africa and in other countries in the world.

This paper aims at bringing up intelligent discussions regarding the instrumentality of social media in initiation, coordination and implementation of social mobilization and campaigns towards influencing government policies and advocating for good governance. With specific reference to the Nigerian youth #EndSARS peaceful protests, the study attempts to explore the power of citizenry in Africa, through the use of social media platforms, to agitate for social, economic, and political transformations within a polity in a peaceful manner.

Drawing critical insights from the efforts of Nigerian youths on the strategic use of social media, this study engages from sources from social media and news reports to understand and explain strategies and mechanisms to influence government policies and decision making through practical usage of social media in the age of digitalization.

Nigerian youths #EndSARS protest: A brief background

The case of Nigeria's #EndSARS draws attention to the problem of police brutality and perpetrations by the Special Anti-Robbery Squad (SARS), a unit of the Nigeria Police Force in Africa's most populous country in particular to the issues of police high-handedness, brutality and errings in Nigeria led to the outburst of the protest both online and offline to seek police accountability and the impact of the mass action and consequences of the EndSARS campaign. Despite the fact that there are different institution channels such the public complaints bureau within the police public relations office, social media handles, police service commission and the police public complaints telephone hotline numbers are available to lodge complaints on police brutality in the country, there is a diverse skepticism among Nigerians that the police authority would not bring its personnel to book for committing professional perpetration as the Nigerian Police Force lacks accountability. Specifically, (Peak, 1997) stated that accountability in police officers is needed for eradicating corruption, imprudent use of force and improving the code of ethics in police departments. The US Agency for International Development (2018) sees police accountability as guaranteeing that police services and their personnel justify the law, respect the rights of the people, and do not engage in wrongdoings, malfeasance or corrupt behaviour.

The #ENDSARS awareness dates back to 2017 when the hashtag appeared on twitter before it gained global momentum in 2020 after SARS officials shot a young man, left him by the roadside and took his Lexus SUV in Ughelli Delta state, Nigeria, on October 3, 2020. The protest came to live after a tweet was made on a twitter handle disseminating information about the incident of the murder. The handler "@AfricaOfficial2" tweeted saying:

"SARS just shot a young boy dead at Ughelli, Delta State as we speak. In front of Wetland hotels. They left him dead on the road side and drove away with the deceased Lexus jeep. I have videos."

The physical movement of the protest started in Lagos from where it actively advanced to other cities and states across the country. Prior to November 2017, organized and coordinated public protests against the Nigeria Police Force were very rare. Thus, the #EndSARS public protest was unprecedented and certainly represents a landmark in the Nigerian sociopolitical space (Ojedokun et al, 2021). The creation of the SARS in 1992 as a division of the Criminal Investigation Department of the Nigeria Police Force (NPF) was seen as a welcome advancement by many Nigerians. The squad was originally set up by the law enforcement agency with the foremost authority of addressing the continuing problem of armed robbery that was confronting the then Nigerian capital city, Lagos (Nnaedozie, 2017). The track record by the first crop of officials of this specialized unit in the execution of their duties over time encouraged the spread of the operation of SARS to other States in Nigeria under the instruction to cover the arrest, investigation and prosecution of suspected kidnappers, murderers, armed robbers, hired assassins, and people involved in other violent crimes (Ojedokun et al, 2021).

3

Adding to the context, the #EndSARS protest constituted major means through which citizens expressed their grievance(s). The #EndSARS protest is synonymous to the Black Lives Matter movement on police brutality in the United States of America. For instance, prior to #EndSARS protest in Nigeria during the month of october, the #blacklivesmatters hashtag was vibrant across various social media platforms to raise awareness for the deaths of breonna Taylor and George floyd who were both victims of police brutality as this was the case in Nigeria where Jimoh Isiaq was killed by the police during the EndSARS protest in Nigeria.

The two weeks of protest in Nigeria and including outside the media landscape of the country was informative with regards to discussions about digital activism and its productiveness in the internet age, as scholars explored the dynamics of symbolic activism (also referred to as clicktivism) and important action that includes public mobilization.

The Special Anti Robbery Squad was created for the purpose of tackling the issue of armed robbery and kidnapping in Nigeria. This unit has been criticized for losing its priorities for killing innocent citizens who are perceived to be perpetrators because of their appearances such as having dreadlocks, wearing crazy jeans and durags, and having earrings on among the male youths and also owning valuable assets like iPhones, cars, MacBook and laptops.

In spite of a few reported victims of police abuse with several investigations including previous attempts to reform the police by the Vice President, Yemi Osinbajo in 2018 which was aborted, the Nigerian government actions have been ineffective (Abimbade et al, 2021). Significantly, a major highlight of the protest was the demands for improved service conditions for police officers. While the Nigerian Police Force struggles to restore a positive representation in the country, the SARS unit has violated its own responsibilities committing abuses targeted to the Nigerian youth population. (Abiodun, 2020), who noted that the abuses perpetrated by SARS were due to absence of emotional intelligence, alcohol and drug abuse especially while on duty, the impeding cases of police reforms in the country and general corruption. SARS officers were generally accused of abuse of power, intimidation, framing up people who didn't commit any crime, extortion, illegal arrest and extrajudicial killings. The male gender were major victims of the perpetrations of this erring officers as they were usually targeted if they are perceived rich based on their appearances. Some of these male victims are forcefully extorted by this officers to the extent that some are arrested and forcefully taken to automated teller machine (ATM) points to make cash withdrawals for them.

Digital mobilization & Fundraising

In times of mobilizing protesters within different states across the country and beyond to meet in different locations, social media played a very important role for the Nigerian youths to achieve these gatherings. Meetings were also called for in Birnin Kudu, Jigawa State; at multiple locations in Lagos State, including at the University of Lagos Front Gate (at 11:00am), Shitta Roundabout in Surulere (at 10:00am), and at Lekki-Ikoyi Bridge (4:00 a. m.) on multiple dates. Abuja youths were also mobilized on October 12 (at 6:00am) at Berger Roundabout and at the Unity Fountain on October 15 (by 7:00am) and in various cities and states in the country. Nigerians in diaspora also actively came out to protest in different cities and countries across the world. Information regarding assembly of protest grounds and mass mobilization were disseminated in the following tweets:

- @YeleSo\nowre- There will be an #EndSARS March in Berlin, Germany on December 10. 2020. please if you live in Germany endeavour to attend! #RevolutionNow
- @bibzyCarter- Today, 24.10.2020. We held our #EndSars Protest in Gottingen, Germany. We stand with every Nigerian to demand good governance and say No to Police Brutality.
- @ECoolOfficial- CHANGE IS NOW!! Atlanta, Thankyou to EVERYONE that came out last minute and in the rain! #ENDSARS
- @Gbemisoke- #EndSARS Houston. Southwest Farmers Market parking lot. Bissonnet @ Centre Pkwy. 2pm. Let's go.
- @asount- Another round of peaceful protests this week in Dallas and Houston against the inhumane treatment of Nigerian citizens. #EndSARS October 21,2020 :
- Fox 4 News Station : 400 N Griffin St Dallas , TX 75202 @ 4pm
- October 24,2020: 9801 Bissonnet st Houston, TX 77036 @ 2pm
- @Cyndodo_- I am so proud of my Generation... see people showed up.. we literally filled the streets of Dallas.. #endsars
- @aireyys- I want to lead the #EndSARS protest here in London, who will join me? Nigerians in the Diaspora let's not be silent #EndSARS #EndSarsProtests
- @OgbeniDipo- On 11/10/2020, alongside other young Nigerians, we led an #EndSARS protest in London, UK in solidarity with our fellow citizens back home in Nigeria. We deployed our resources, time, and money to make our voices heard. And indeed, the global media paid attention to #ENDSARS

- @ABUJAPLUG- #SARSMUSTEND Peaceful Protest in Abuja. Date: Monday, 12th October, 2020, Time: 6am, Venue1: Berger Roundabout (Under the bridge), Venue2: City Gate, Abuja
- @UnclePamilerin- If you are around Akoka or Yaba, we lend our voice today. 11am Unilag Gate. #Endsars #EndSarsProtest #EndSarsNow
- @vobevibes- Tomorrow 11AM Unilag gate. If you live around let's do this together. Let's lend our own voice to this menace that's eating deep into our lives #ENDSARS
- @FakhuusHashim- There are protests in Jigawa on Monday in Birnin Kudu. #EndSARS

One remarkable aspect of the protest which is really commendable was how Nigerian youths were able to raise funds to keep the protest on going. Zald and Ash (1966), they asserted that fundraising is substantial for the encouragement of social protest as it is needed to carry out mobilizations and support its members. During the protest, social media served as a space as it aided the contributions and support which included first aid treatment, food packages for protesters and mobilization of funds especially through Twitter platform. One of the donors supported the movement with a donation of about N1,216,080 to eleven (11) protesters, while stating that they paid the hospital bills of three (3) protesters that were injured and donated to the family of a deceased protester, as well as providing other necessary supplies. He also noted that a total of N62, 643, 663 was raised out of which N13,026, 580 had been spent on the protest (Abimbade et al, 2021). Former CEO of Twitter, Jack Partrick Dorsey also facilitated the donation process by tweeting on his handle for the donation of bitcoin. He tweeted saying:

"Donate via #Bitcoin to help #ENDSARS"

The protest which was vibrantly active specifically on twitter with over 28 million tweets bearing the hashtag "#ENDSARS" led to the creation of the special emoji "a tight fist" in the Nigerian national flag colours (green, white and green). The emoji was created by Jack Dorsey the former CEO of Twitter.

Social media impacts

The relevance of social media in mass protest and activism is very substantial. Social media platforms like Twitter shape political participation, especially during demonstrations. Social media platforms make it possible for informations that are crucial to the execution of protest activities such as informations about turn out, medical services and legal support to be disseminated online as this was the case during the #EndSARS protest. In addition social media fosters the exchange of emotional and motivational contents in support of activism including messages portraying anger, concerns about accountability, fairness, justice and deprivation. Nevertheless, the use of social media has been connected to the spread of political protest in many cities around the world, including Kiev, Moscow, Ankara, Istanbul, Cairo, Tripoli, Madrid, Athens, Los Angeles, New York, Hong Kong, and Ferguson, Missouri. Noticeably, political protest itself is far from new, but the fact that it is possible to access real-time accounts of protest behavior documented and archived through microblogging (e.g., Twitter) and social media (e.g., Facebook) websites is a recent phenomenon. Indeed, it is becoming increasingly difficult to find a protest that does not have its own distinctive hashtag on Twitter (e.g., #OWS 5 Occupy Wall Street; #Jan25 5 protests in Egypt; #direngeziparkı 5 protests in Turkey; and #Euromaidan 5 protests in Ukraine), and it is easy to connect these hashtags to message content, user metadata, and social networks (Jost et al, 2018). (Shirky, 2011) concluded that as the communications landscape gets denser, more complex, and more participatory, the connected population is gaining more access to information, more opportunities to involve themselves in public speech, and an enhanced ability to undertake collective action. (McGarty et al, 2013) asserted that social media usage largely contributes to an acceleration of processes that normally occur much more slowly.

With the advent of social media as an alternative form of mass communication, people can disseminate information freely and diversely as this was the case during the #EndSARS protest. Also, the Nigerian Police Force were able to disseminate it's press release and activities during the protest. The citizens were also able to disseminate information on social media with specific interest in trends on police brutality and digital mobilization. (Carty, 2015), who propounded that social media aids the quick dissemination of information and mobilizes the public for physical protests. Social movement coordination that want to mobilize for a mass street demonstration make substantial use of the internet to enhance arrangements and mobilization endeavors (Van Laer and Van Aelst, 2010). Nigerian youths have become more politically aware and primarily depend on social media to air their views, express, seek, receive, communicate and disseminate information. Particularly, to a new era for political struggle with many Nigerian youths protesting against police brutality. Citizens have delivered strong criticisms towards the government using actual protests and social media at the same time. This has been attained by support across the country and beyond the media landscape of Nigeria as sustained and crucial political activism has been engendered by developing strong ties and relationships on social media with internet users from different geopolitical spaces across

Nigeria. During the protest, many online protesters developed alliances by disseminating circumstances surrounding the protest across various states in the country such as venue of the protest and the time to assemble for the protest. Also, friendships developed among netizens by requesting follow-backs, retweeting their business posts and making donations. Social media has been a very important medium of communication for people to discuss and advocate for good governance in society as this was the case during the #EndSARS protest among Nigerian youths. The democratic nature of social media made it possible for the Nigerian youths to vibrantly discourage police brutality especially when public needs are not met. This was demonstrated in the engagements the Nigerian youths had on Twitter using the hashtag "#EndSARS" to call against police brutality and seeking police accountability.

Methodology

This research was essentially a case-study analysis of the vibrant #EndSARS online and offline protest against police brutality and high-handedness in Nigeria, Africa's most populous country. Data was primarily sourced from twitter where the movement started online and media reports on the subject matter. The Twitter Advanced Search was used to search and filter out tweets that contain keywords or hashtags indicating the activism. The hashtag considered in the search include #ENDSARS, #SARSMUSTGO, #ENDPOLICEBRUTALITY, #ENDSARSNOW, and #SARSMUSTEND. These tweets also produced words and phrases such as protest, celebrities, police brutality, corruption, bribery and freedom. Although the #EndSARS protest finally climaxed in the city of Lagos from where it spread to other states and cities in Nigeria between 3 October and 23 October 2020, the inception of the movement dates back to 2017 when the hashtag first appeared on Twitter. Thus, conscious attempt was made to also cover the events and circumstances that eventually led to the outburst of the October 2020 mass protest. Categorically, news reports on the activities of #EndSARS protesters, the reaction of the Nigeria Police Force and its personnel to the protest, as well as the response of the Nigerian government to the public protest and the demands of the protesters was carefully searched, filtered, read and analysed.

Discussions and Findings

Human Rights Violations by SARS

SARS was created in 1992 as a response to tackle violent crimes in particular to armed robbery and kidnapping. This police unit of the Nigerian Police Force has come to be known for its high-handed tactics and violations of human rights. Wrong doings cut across a range of human rights including the right to life, freedom from torture, right to a fair trial, right to privacy, and freedom of assembly, all of which are rights guaranteed and protected by the Nigerian constitution.

a. Right to Life

Violations of the right to life have come in various forms such as extrajudicial killings, shooting at protesters, and other random, unprovoked killings. The Open Society Justice Initiative (OSJI) found in a 2010 report that extrajudicial executions are regular occurrences of policing in Nigeria (Open Society Justice Initiative, 2010). Human Rights Watch estimated that over 10,000 people have been killed by the Nigerian police Force within eight years spanning 2000 through 2007 (Human Rights Watch, 2007). The head of the Enugu State division of SARS apparently told a researcher of the Network on Police Reform in Nigeria that he instructed the extrajudicial killings of people whom he knew to be guilty (Open Society Justice Initiative). These killings do not always happen in confined spaces. In August 2019, videos emerged revealing men of the Nigerian police force executing arrested suspects in the streets of Lagos (Punch, 2019). The suspects were accused to belong to a criminal group that disguised themselves as phone buyers to lure and rob victims. The police arrested two of the suspects, only to have their execution recorded shortly after. Amateur clips of the police officers shooting the victims to the openness of the public went viral across various social media platforms and broadcast news. In reacting to the whole situation of the incident the Nigerian police announced the arrest of the officers involved.

b. Freedom from torture

SARS personnel have also been infamous to regularly torture suspects for "confessions." The OSJI report states that the practice is so common that many police stations have a person on staff who is in charge to torture detainees and a room set aside for this conduct. police officers even have their own slangs they use to communicate among themselves for various methods of torture (Open Society Justice Initiative). Amnesty International has also recorded cases of torture, most of which originated from detainees in SARS custody (Amnesty International, 2016). The police usually use various forms of brutality, including sexual violence on detainees and suspects. Others describe being shot in limbs, assaulted by police officers while in prison, having multiple fractures, or being forced to perform painful exercises. Sex workers in particular report being raped by police officers (Reuters, 2019). In February 2020, BBC Africa published an excruciating documentary titled "The Torture Virus: Tabay 'rampant' among

Nigeria's security forces". The video revealed the use of an execution known as Tabay. The execution involves tying up detainees in a crude and painful fashion: the arms are forced back and tied at the elbows, cutting circulation to the hands and disabling the victim from moving. The feet are then tied back, arching the spine and deforming the body into a triangle. Some of the victims are hung above a fire then a heavy block usually a wood or concrete, is often mounted on the victim's back to aggravate the pain. In the documentary, a man identified as a Nigerian police officer gives a distressful account of the use of Tabay by SARS: "They call it 'Hawan Keke' (bicycle ride). I have witnessed it often. The room is dark. Your hands are tied up from behind. If it is not tight enough, the elbows are tied in a way that stops the blood from circulating. Your legs are tied to a chair so you cannot move. In the documentary he revealed that SARS officers torture victims in whatever way they want either by beating or electrocution.

c. Right to Liberty

SARS, as well as other units of the Nigerian Police, regularly detain suspects, sometimes for years without trial. The average years of pre-trial detention in Nigeria is three years and ten months (Open Society Justice Initiative). Such delayed detentions are usually done through the use of a "holding charge," whereby the police bring a charge against an accused before a lower court lacking jurisdiction to try the crime, impending advice from the Director of Public Prosecutions. The Nigerian Court has held this conduct to be unconstitutional, though this practice still continues.

d. Right to privacy and family life

SARS personnel, ironically hired to curtail and tackle violent crimes, have recently assumed the mandate of fishing out so-called "Yahoo boys" (internet fraudsters). This they do by stopping young men in the streets and forcefully demanding to go through their phones and other gadgets. Mere ownership of an iPhone is enough to perceive a young man a suspect. Victims on several occasions have reported being arrested for owning iPhones and laptops or for refusing to grant police officers access to their phones (Forbes Africa, 2020).

Activism

Activism is protest. According to Oxford learners dictionary activism is the activity of working to achieve political or social change, especially as a member of an organization with particular aims. Marchetti (2016) defines activism as acting in direct opposition of a policy. Hands (2011) details that activism can be understood within the context of strong difference of opinion, which is a state of indicating strong displeasure, resistance which involves taking actions to avert distressing situations from iterating. In summary, people protest when they are infuriated (Castells, 2015). Since the advent of social media, activists in Africa have vibrantly used the affordances to bypass established systems and ask for change (Mutsvairo, 2016). As Castells (2015) suggests, the internet has provided the tools the people need to mobilize others and act on their grievances and anger. By this, it can be concluded to call participants of the #EndSARS campaign activists

The Nigerian youth #EndSARS peaceful protests and international empathy.

The #EndSARS protests evoked global empathy and support, with world leaders such as United Nations Secretary-General António Guterres and Former United States Secretary of State Mike Pompeo tweeting in support. Other political figures and celebrities also used the hashtag or referenced the movement to either support the protests or demand an end to the government crackdown on protestors. These includes the United States of America president Joe Biden, former United States Secretary of State Hillary Clinton, boxing heavyweight champion Anthony Joshua, Former Arsenal footballer Mesut Ozil, and American rapper Kanye West. For several days in October, the hashtag #EndSARS was a vibrant trending topic on global Twitter. Beyond the media landscape of Nigeria, some international celebrities which include Trey Songz, Big Sean, Chance The Rapper, Estelle, Nasty C also lent their voices to the raging protests in Nigeria.

Celebrity influencers as digital vanguard

The demographic category of protesters who engaged in the protest were basically the millennial population of Nigeria, that is, people born in the 1980s, 1990s, or early 2000s, which also includes the age range of celebrities who were also involved in the protest both home and abroad. Names, location, profile pictures, twitter handles, and the language of tweets were used to determine the nationality. During the protest Nigerian youths were not apprehensive to accept coercion. As a result of the protest they were called the "Sorosoke generation". Sorosoke here means (Be audible/Speak up). The Nigerian youths activism on twitter during the protest was also captured via the viral hashtag #sorosoke, a phrase that was derived from a yoruba nollywood movie and attributed to the celebrity, Toyin Afolayan who is an actress. This phrase was introduced into the struggle while the Lagos State Governor, Babajide Sanwo-Olu addressed the protesters in the Lekki area, as they persuaded him to be audible. This case brought up the assertion that celebrities influence on social media was vital in navigating and sustaining the Nigerian youths vibrancy towards the phenomenon.

The Nigerian youths called out celebrities to fervently take part in the protest both online and offline. These celebrities included pastors, artistes, nollywood actors and actresses and other social media influencers. As (Hanks, 2019) emphasized, youths organize themselves within wide social movement groups by creating a sphere of influence within their age group and this was expressed in the emergence of youth celebrities into leadership positions during the #EndSARS protest. The protests featured individuals like Folarin Falana (FALZ), Obianuju Catherine Udeh (DJ Switch), Douglas Jack Agu (Runtown), Michael Collins Ajereh (Don Jazzy), Debo Adedayo (Mr Macaroni), Temitope Savage(Tiwa Savage), Adekunle Almoruf Kosoko, (Adekunle Gold), Peter Okoye (Mr. P), Chinedu Okoli (Flavor), David Adeleke (Davido), Pastor Sam Adeyemi, Ayodeji Balogun (Wizkid), Simisola Bolatito Kosoko (Simi), Shoneye Olamilekan, Lala Dapo, Funke Etti, and Seyi Edun among others who played substantial roles both on social media and protest venues. Adding to this, Ayodeji Balogun (Wizkid) was the first Nigerian celebrity to actively come online to condemn police brutality among the youths in the country. He remarkably tagged the President and blasted him on his tweet. He tweeted:

" @MBuhari you are a failure! Old and incompetent! Step down! We don't want you, your Vice President and your IG! Resign !." He also replied a women who perceived his tweet as being disrespectful to the president saying:

"lol a 77 year old man is not young ma.. You are a woman and a mother and kids are getting killed by police/sars and this is all you have to say? shame on you!!! shame on you!! I am a father and age has nothing to do with demanding for a better governance in my country!!"

Nigerian youths on twitter aimed at those celebrities who initially failed to involve themselves at the beginning of the protest. They threatened to unfollow their handles, stop streaming their songs, thereby reducing their sphere of influence. For example, Daniel Oluwatobiloba Anidugbe (Kizz Daniel), Damini Ogulu (Burna Boy), and Florence Otedola (DJ Cuppy) were backlashed for not joining the protests during its early stages in the following tweets:

- @Izu_fcb- But why has @burnaboy decided not to say anything concerning this #EndSARS issue?
- @ghaffarr_b- I'm a huge burna boy Stan and him not saying anything about this #EndSARS issue is so disappointing

- @Yemihazan- The youths with no connections & parents connected to high places will always be at the receiving end, not trying to insinuate anything but I remember DJ Cuppy tweeted severally on black life matters but haven't seen any post #EndSARS from her, considering her influence here
- @Mayorshef- Kizz Daniel never post anything about the #EndSARS movement. Shame!

They subsequently joined the movement after they were called out. Burna Boy supported the movement by mounting #EndSARS billboards across the country to create awearness of the protest against the notorious police unit the Special Anti-Robbery Squad (SARS). He tweeted on his official Twitter handle "@burnaboy", "My #EndSARS billboards have gone up all over Nigeria."

ENDSARS Protest and the Positive Impacts of Protesting Police Misconduct in Nigeria

The first major impact of the protest was that SARS was eventually disbanded by the then Inspector General of Police, Muhammed Adamu, due to the tenacity of the protesters both home and abroad. The disbandment took place on 11 October 2020. The Federal Government of Nigeria stated that a special presidential directive had ordered the immediate dissolution of the Special Anti-Robbery Squad (SARS) as the information was disseminated on Twitter by the Presidency of Nigeria twitter handle "@NGRPresident" in the following tweet:

"PRESIDENTIAL DIRECTIVE: The Special Anti-Robbery Squad (SARS) of the Nigeria Police Force @PoliceNG has been dissolved WITH IMMEDIATE EFFECT. The Inspector General of Police will communicate further developments in this regard. All officers and men of the now defunct Special Anti-Robbery Squad (SARS) are to be redeployed with immediate effect. A new policing arrangement to address anticipated policing gaps the dissolution of SARS will cause is being worked on and will be announced by @PoliceNG."

Secondly, the EndSARS campaign was able to create awareness on police abuse, perpetrations and brutality across various cities and states in Nigeria and beyond the media landscape in the country. Adding to the phenomenon, the campaign also increased public enlightenments as regards to right of the citizens to seek good governance against police brutality and to make officers accountable for their errings through social media which police officers are aware of that their actions and perpetrations towards a citizen can be recorded and disseminated on social media which could lead to an issue of public discussion across various social media platforms.

Thirdly, the protest also gained momentum as SARS officers who were accused of police brutality and high-handedness were arrested and prosecuted. Owing to the intense pressure exerted on the Nigeria Police Force by the mass action, some ex-SARS officials found culpable of engaging in professional misconduct were made accountable for their actions. As this was the case on 20 October 2020, a Presidential Investigative Panel on SARS charged with the responsibility of investigating the allegations of human rights violations levelled against officers of the unit recommended the dismissal of 35 SARS officials from the Nigeria Police Force, the prosecution of 33 personnel, and the demotion of 23 others (Ikhilae, 2020). Similarly, the intensity and scope of the mass action orchestrated by the #EndSARS protest also compelled some governors to individually inaugurate a Judicial Panel of Inquiry to investigate cases of police brutality and other extrajudicial acts committed by officials of the disbanded police detachment in their respective state (This Day, 2020; Vanguard, 2020).

Lastly, one of the major reasons why protesters took to the streets was the demand for police officers to be adequately paid in Nigeria so as to avoid extortion from the masses. So therefore, a remarkable impact of the protest was that the protesters persuaded the Nigerian government to revamp the Nigerian Police Force and to improve the working conditions of police personnel as President Muhammadu Buhari in a national broadcast on 22 October 2020 directed the National Salaries, Income, and Wages Commission to immediately design a new salary structure for officials of the Nigeria Police Force.

Negative Impact of the #EndSARS Protest for Policing and Law Enforcement in Nigeria

It turns out that the protest had some some consequences on policing and law enforcement in Nigeria and implications as discussed in this section. After the protest, the West African Network for Peace Building (WANEP) recorded at least 78 extrajudicial killings and 73 injuries resulting from the protest which was hijacked by unethical individuals between October 17 and 21, 2020 to disrupt protesters which led to the breakdown of law and order across various cities in the country leaving many parts of states in the country with burnt buildings, looted shops and destroyed properties. The beginning of the protest was initially peaceful not until reports of violence against protesters who were beaten and tear gassed by police at the National Assembly Complex in Abuja and also at the Lekki Toll Gate in Lagos State and the killing of Jimoh Isiaka in Oyo State. What began as peaceful protest turned catastrophic on October 20, when the Nigerian military opened fire at the Lekki tollgate, in

Lagos State killing innocent protesters. According to Amnesty International, military officers killed thirty-eight protesters, in what was called "the Lekki Massacre" (Columbia Journalism Review, 2020).

Notable protesters were also killed during the activism process. For instance the death of Oke, a graduate of computer science from the Federal University of Agriculture, Abeokuta, who was killed by thugs during the protest. Oke died at the age 21. Few hours before Oke was killed, he tweeted on his handle "@O_Okee" saying:

"Nigeria will not end me." Also the death of a mechanic who was killed while he had both hands in his pockets during the protest at Surulere, Lagos State and the protesters at the Lekki Toll Gate were disseminated in the following tweets:

@Tbabz__- "The man that was shot in Surulere had both his hands in his pocket. Still does. He was clearly a bystander and not protesting yet the Police shot him. If somehow you still think this cannot be any one of us, you're dead wrong. #ENDSARS! #SARSMUSTEND!"

@kizitopng- "This man is a mechanic that works on my street. He went to get a car from a customer then at #surulere, around barracks he got stuck in traffic and came out to see what was happening and got hit by a stray bullet. #EndSarsNow #EndPoliceBrutality #SURULEREPROTEST #SARSMUSTEND."

@SavvyRinu- "Jimoh Isiaq was killed by the Nigerian Police in Oyo State for standing meters away from the ongoing #EndSARS protest this time last year. I pray we never forget the way this murderous government went after peaceful protesters."

@Mayorspeaks- "BREAKING: Massive Gunshot at Lekki Toll Gate at the moment as the military men shoot at #EndSARS Protesters.
#EndPoliceBrutalityinNigera."

@Annie_Ojuolape- "Took off the CCTV cameras and Put off the lights at Lekki tollgate, Brought armour tanks and released life bullets on #EndSARS Peaceful protesters whose only weapon was the National Flag? History will never forget."

@TimiDollars- "20/10/2020 Lekki Tollgate Massacre by the Government. The Nigerian army shot peaceful protesters who simply carried flags. We would never forget!"

@Auntyadaa- "I woke up thinking about so many things. I woke up thinking about Jimoh, Oke, the lady that was shot in the mouth, the man that died with both hands in his pocket, the people that were shot at holding the flag of Nigeria. Are these people going to die for nothing? #ENDSARS."

Seventeen police stations were burnt in Lagos state, the oldest court in Nigeria was burnt. The home of the Lagos state governor, Babajide Sanwo-Olu was also burnt. The headquarters of Television Continental (TVC) a media outlet was set ablaze while the office of The Nation newspaper was also wrecked. Bus terminals were burnt and destroyed in several parts of Lagos state. The office of the Nigerian Ports Authority (NPA) in Lagos was also set ablaze by hoodlums. The dockyard at Apapa was attacked, valuable items were stolen by the hoodlums, and vehicles and other properties set ablaze (Premium Times, 2020). Covid-19 warehouses storing palliatives and provisions were also invaded in various states. These developments led to curfews imposed by various state governments in the country. This incident is compared to (Reynolds-Stenson, 2017) who stated that protest against police brutality is very likely to lead to widespread confrontations, property damage, and violence. The protest also led to some encounters between police officers and protesters which led to the death of some persons.

The #EndSARS protest also negatively hindered the Nigerian government's efforts at controlling the spread of the virus infection. As a result of the protest, people involved in the public protest engaged in acts that constituted a violation of the Nigeria Centre for Disease Control's prescribed health protocols for COVID-19. Apart from the fact that the protesters in contravention of the federal government imposed mass gathering restriction order routinely converged in large numbers during the public protest, many of the protesters also protested without wearing any protective gear such as nose masks or face shields (Sobowale, 2020).

Safety Challenges for Journalist and Press Restriction

The Nigerian Broadcasting Commission (NBC), Nigeria's media regulator, in a press release urged media outlets to disseminate incidents of the protest and attacks with caution, and to refrain from doing anything that would embarrass the Nigerian government and the country. As a result of restrictions on reporting events involving the protest, depending on TV news broadcast was not enough for the Nigerian youths which made social media become prominent as the main source of information as political officials aimed to control informations and contents disseminated by traditional media which are more likely to disseminate messages in support of the government. Nigerian citizens during the protest had diverse beliefs that the Nigerian media did not effectively cover the reports and circumstances during the protest which resulted to the masses depending on social media as various media outlets incompetently performed their surveillance functions. Some perceived that the government influenced the coverage of reports as journalists where being attacked during the protest.

According to Reporters Without Borders in their annual release of the press freedom index of 2020, Nigeria ranked 115th out of 180 countries. The Nigerian media has a history of being backlashed by military regimes with intent on harassing, killing, intimidation, imprisoning and murdering of journalists. The 2020 edition of the index evaluates the situations for journalists across 180 countries and territories because of factors affecting journalism such as aggressiveness of authoritarian regimes, democratic crisis and economic crisis impoverishing the quality of journalism (Reporters Without Borders, 2020). President Muhammadu Buhari, a former military dictator between the years of 1983 to 1985 was democratically elected into power in the presidential election of 2015. With the occurrence of media restrictions during the protest, many perceived and viewed the incident a repetition of his old regime which was characterized with fear, violence, harassment and prosecution of the press (Columbia Journalism Review, 2020).

Human beings are entitled to certain rights irrespective of gender, status, race, religion, political affiliation, level of education and level of income. In a society, the people have the right to protest and journalist who cover reports and events surrounding such protest also have the right to be protected from intimidation, harassment and other risk factors involving the job. Nigeria has a long history of human rights abuses perpetrated by the Nigerian Military. For instance, in 1999, when the Nigerian military invaded Udi a community in Bayelsa State where many innocent civilians were killed. Also, in 2001, The Nigerian military invaded Zaki Biam in Benue State which led to the death of people in the process. The Nigerian military again in 2017, invaded a local government area in Benue State called Naka, and killed many civilians and homes burnt down.

Journalist need to feel safe in discharging their duties whilst acting as watchdogs of the society. (Maslow, 1943) who classified safety needs in his social order of needs as he classified safety as the second layer of people needs. Also (Burleson and Thoron, 2017) in discussing the importance of safety in their study noted that "If a child has a bad home life (fighting parents, addicted parents, absent parents, etc.) or lives in an unsafe neighborhood, the child will have trouble focusing on learning when he/ she does not feel secure." With those words, Burleson and Thoron paint a brief picture of the importance of safety in human behaviour. Therefore, within the framework of Maslow's theory of human motivation, it can be affirmed that journalists' safety is an important motivational factor that could influence their job execution. Journalist just like other humans have the right to feel safe, as well as their family members. They need to be sure that their place of work is not a dead zone and also their beat, that is a specific location assigned to them while reporting is safe (Talabi et al, 2021).

During the protest, journalist as watchdogs of the society tried their possible best to provide day to day information surrounding the protest. According to (Akinfeleye, 2009), He stated that a journalist is watchdog of the public; his role is like a dog that is kept to guard a house and giving warning of the approach of intruders or invaders. The role of the journalist in this direction is to watch over the interests of the people and to bark if and when these interests are threatened. He is the crusader of social justice, public morality, civil liberties and human progress. This led to them facing a lot of risks. For instance, a journalist (Cameraman) with Arise TV, Francis Ogbonna while covering the #EndSars protest on a sunday in Abuja was attacked by the Nigerian police (Independent, 2020). Also according to premium times in a news report, The Committee to Protect Journalists (CPJ) stated 12 journalists and five media outlets were attacked during the EndSARS protests (Premium Times, 2020). A Premium time journalist, Ebuka Onyeji, was also assaulted by police officers while covering the #EndSARS protest in Abuja (Premium Times, 2020). The National Broadcasting Commission (NBC), Nigeria's media regulator sanctioned major broadcast stations for violating broadcasting code during the #ENDSARS protests. They included Channels Television, African Independent Television and Arise TV; all fined 3 million naira each (Vanguard, 2020).

Reporting protest is a part of conflict reporting because protest is a sign of conflict. People protest because they face injustice that their government failed to solve. The aim of protesting is to create awareness of a particular unresolved issue. Protest can be viewed as a communication strategy through which people with similar objectives express themselves (Talabi et al, 2021). Covenant on Civil and Political Rights in its articles 19 and 21 as it is clear that engaging in peaceful protests is vital demonstration of the rights to freedom of peaceful assembly and freedom of expression. Furthermore, general comment No. 34 (2011) of the Human Rights Committee, notes that freedom of opinion and freedom of expression are pivotal prerequisites needed for the complete development of a person and are equally essential for the amelioration of democracy (United Nations, 2013). So therefore, safety must be guaranteed for journalist when covering news stories on protest and conflicts as they fulfill their duties in safeguarding freedom of expression and human rights.

Conclusion

The article demonstrates how Nigeria youths political consciousness and shared interests became clear tools to fight police brutality on social media and in physical protests. Social media was used as a public sphere to participate in political discussions, mobilize and create identities. The research examined the various protest strategies adopted by the youth activists such as calling out celebrities, unfollowing political leaders, sharing stories, news reports and tweets and fundraising in less than one month of mobilization and protests. The implications of this participation was seen in the Government's decision to abolish SARS and set up judicial panels of inquiry and investigation. The study proves the fact that social media is important to foster digital activism geared at influencing change in the political sphere in Nigeria and Africa as a whole.

Reference

Abimbabe, O. et al. (2022). Millennial activism within Nigerian Twitterscape: From mobilization to social action of #ENDSARS protest. Social Sciences & Humanities Open, 6(1), 100-222. https://doi.org/10.1016/j.ssaho.2021.100222

Abiodun, T. (2020). Unlawful killings of civilians by officers of the special anti-robbery Squad (SARS) unit of the Nigerian police in southwest Nigeria: Implications for national security. African Journal of Law, Political Research and Administration, 3(1), 49-64.

Akinfeleye, R. (2009) Media Nigeria. Nelson Publishers Limited, Lagos.

Amnesty International. (September 21, 2016). Nigeria: 'You have signed your death warrant' : Torture and other ill treatment in the Special Anti-Robbery Squad. https://www.amnesty.org/en/documents/afr44/4868/2016/en/

Burleson S and Thoron A (2017) Maslow's hierarchy of needs and its relation to learning and achievement. Retrieved from https://edis.ifas.ufl.edu/pdffiles/WC/ WC15900.pdf.

Carty, V. (2015). Social Movements and New Technology.

Castells, M. (2015). Networks of outrage and hope: Social movements in the internet age. Cambridge, UK: Polity Press.

Columbia Journalism Review. (November 2, 2020). Nigeria's #EndSARS Movement and Media Suppression. https://www.cjr.org/analysis/nigeria-endsars-press-freedom.php

Forbes Africa. (October 13, 2020). Nigeria Dissolves SARS But The Youth Demand Justice. https://www.forbesafrica.com/current-affairs/2020/10/13/nigeria-dissolves-sars-but-the-youth-demand-justice/

Hands, J. (2011). @ is for activism: Dissent, resistance and rebellion in a digi- tal culture. London, UK: Pluto Press.

Hank, J. (2019). The elephant in the room: Youth, cognition, and student groups in mass social movements. Societies, 9(55), 1–19.

Human Rights Watch. (November 18, 2007). Nigeria: Investigate Widespread Killings by Police https://www.hrw.org/news/2007/11/18/nigeria-investigate-widespread-killings-police

Ikhilae, E. (October 20, 2020). Presidential Panel Recommends Dismissal of 35 SARS Officials, Prosecution of 33. The Nation.

Independent. (October 11, 2020). BREAKING: Police Brutalise Arise TV Cameraman While Covering Protest In Abuja. https://independent.ng/breaking-police-brutalise-arise-tv-cameraman-while-covering-protest-in-abuja/

Jost, T. et al. (2018) How Social Media Facilitates Political Protest: Information, Motivation, and Social Networks. Political psychology, 39(1), 85-118. https://doi.org/10.1111/pops.12478

Marchetti, G. (2016). Activism. Journal of Chinese Cinemas, 10(1), 4–37.

Maslow AH (1943) A theory of human motivation. Psychological Review 50(4): 370–396.

McGarty, C., Thomas, E. F., Lala, G., Smith, L. G., & Bliuc, A. M. (2013). New technologies, new identities, and the growth of mass opposition in the Arab Spring. Political Psychology, 35(6), 725–740.

Mutsvairo, B. (2016). Dovetailing desires for democracy with new ICTs' potentiality as platform for activism. In B. Mutsvairo (Ed.), Digital activism in the social media era (pp. 3–23). Cham, Switzerland: Palgrave Macmillan.

Nnaedozie, E. (23 Dec, 2017). How I Founded SARS in the Police –RTD CP Midenda. Vanguard.

Ojedokun, U.et al. (2021) Mass mobilization for police accountability: The case of Nigeria's #EndSARS protest. Policing, 15(1), 1894-1903. https://doi.org/10.1093/police/paab001

Open Society Justice Initiative, supra note 5. https://www.justiceinitiative.org/publications/criminal-force-torture-abuse-and-extrajudicial-killings-nigeria-police-force

Open Society Justice Initiative, supra note 5 at 22. https://www.justiceinitiative.org/publications/criminal-force-torture-abuse-and-extrajudicial-killings-nigeria-police-force

Open Society Justice Initiative, supra note 5 at 7. https://www.justiceinitiative.org/publications/criminal-force-torture-abuse-and-extrajudicial-killings-nigeria-police-force

Peak, K. (1997). Policing America: Methods, Issues, Challenges. Upper Saddle River: New Jersey: Prentice Hall.

Premium Times. (October 29, 2020). #ENDSARS: 12 journalists, five media outlets attacked during protests – CPJ. https://www.premiumtimesng.com/news/top-news/423650-endsars-12-journalists-five-media-outlets-attacked-during-protests-cpj.html

Premium Times. (October 11, 2020). #EndSARS: Police attack PREMIUM TIMES journalist covering Abuja protest. https://www.premiumtimesng.com/news/top-news/419991-endsars-police-attack-premium-times-journalist-covering-abuja-protest.html

Premium Times. (October 25, 2020). How hoodlums took advantage of #EndSARS, wreaked havoc in Lagos. https://www.premiumtimesng.com/news/headlines/422983-how-hoodlums-took-advantage-of-endsars-wreaked-havoc-in-lagos.html

Punch. (August 20, 2019). Policemen shoot dead suspected phone thieves in Lagos. https://punchng.com/sars-operatives-shoot-dead-suspected-phone-thieves-in-lagos/

Reporters Without Borders. 2020 World Press Freedom Index: "Entering a decisive decade for journalism, exacerbated by coronavirus". https://rsf.org/en/2020-world-press-freedom-index-entering-decisive-decade-journalism-exacerbated-coronavirus

Reuters. (May 6, 2016). Nigerian police accused of abusing prostitution suspects. https://www.reuters.com/article/us-nigeria-police-women-idUSKCN1SC1KD

Reynolds-Stenson, H. (2017). Protesting the Police: Anti-Police Brutality Claims as a Predictor of Police Repression of Protest. Social Movement Studies, 17(1), 48-63. https://doi.org/10.1080/14742837.2017.1381592

Shirky, C. (2011). The political power of social media. Foreign Affairs, 90, 28–41.

Sobowale, R. (October 27, 2020). Nigeria: COVID-19 Infections Likely to Rise Due to Large Gatherings, NCDC Boss Warns. Sahara Reporters.

Talabi, O. et al. (2021) Modeling safety challenges journalists faced in reporting anti-police brutality protests (ENDSARS protests) in Nigeria. Sage Journals. https://doi.org/10.1177/02666669211054367

This Day. (October 20, 2020). Sanwo-Olu, Okowa, Obaseki, El-Rufai, Others Inaugurate Police Brutality Panels. https://www.thisdaylive.com/index.php/2020/10/20/sanwo-olu-okowa-obaseki-el-rufai-others-inaugurate-police-brutality-panels/amp/

United Nations (2013) Human Rights Council Twenty-second session Agenda items 2 and 3 Annual report of the United Nations High Commissioner for Human Rights and reports of the Office of the High Commissioner and the Secretary- General. Retrieved from https://www.ohchr.org/Documents/ HRBodies/HRCouncil/RegularSession/Session22/A.HRC.22.28.pdf.

United States Agency for International Development.
(2018). The Effectiveness of Police Accountability Mech- anisms: What Works and the Way Ahead. USAID.
https://www.usaid.gov>gsearch>accountability.

Vanguard. (October 26, 2020). #ENDSARS Coverage: Why we fined AIT, Channels, Arise TV, N3m each — NBC. https://www.vanguardngr.com/2020/10/endsars-coverage-why-we-fined-ait-channels-arise-tv-n3m-each-%E2%80%95-nbc/amp/

Vanguard. (October 24, 2020). #EndSARS: Niger Govt. Inaugurates 14-Man Judicial Panel of Inquiry. https://www.vanguardngr.com/2020/10/endsars-niger-govt-inaugurates-14-man-judicial-panel-of-inquiry/amp/

Van Laer, J., & Van Aelst, P. (2010). Internet and social movement action repertoires. Information, Communication & Society, 13(8), 1146–1171. https://doi.org/10.1080/13691181003628307

Zald, M., & Ash, R. (1966). Social movement organisations: Growth, decay and change. Social Forces, 44(3), 327–341.